to the World's best
Grandpa

edited by Helen Exley

≋EXLEY

The happy one

I love you grandad because you make me laugh.

MELISSA PURDY, AGE 8

I love my grandad very much. With his white hair, chubby face and warming smile he always looks very happy. We visit him every Saturday and Sunday and he always looks pleased to see us. I love my grandad, he's really my number one.

KAREN MOONEY, AGE 11

My grandpa is always nice. Whenever he sees me he welcomes me with open arms and a smiling face.

WINSTON, AGE 9

He fills
my life
with
happiness

JAYESH, AGE 9

KAREN McKEE

He's helpful
in times of
trouble. If
we ever need
him he'll
be there

JAMES O'NEILL

MICHAELAE MOORE,
AGE 9

He understands

We need our grandfathers because they understand us when we have got problems.

RHEA GRANT, AGE 10

I love you because you put plasters on me when I'm hurt.

VANESSA COPPOCK, AGE 9½

I love you because you take care of me and play with me when I am lonely.

JULIE KIRK, AGE 7

What are Grandpas?

They might look old,
but there's something
inside them, that
makes you happy,
and want to be beside
them, they are a
bubble of fun
inside everyone,
that makes you want
to be, beside them.
Now, that's a
grandpa!

PAUL LODGE, AGE 11¼

Even though they might go on about how things used to be, they still care and still worry, sometimes too much. You're their grandchild, whatever you can say. It will always, always be that way.

RUTH BUNYAN, AGE 12

REBECCA LAMBERT, AGE 7

You are like a
pal to me.

TRACEY-ANNE
ANDREWS,
AGE 10½

ANDREW ROWE
AGE 9

My pal

I think my grandpa is the best in the world. He gives me rides on the tractor when we are picking potatoes. I like it when I get to feed the cows with turnips, and I love feeding the pet lambs with the milk bottle. I like it when he takes me up on his knee and reads me a story. I like it when we play snap and I win.

NEIL REID, AGE 6

My Grandpa can do Popeye by taking his false teeth out

JULIE ANN
TRAINOR,
AGE 10

PHILIP MARSH
AGE 7

falling to bits

I like my grandpa because he takes his false teeth out and pretends to bite my baby sister.

JOLENE KELLY, AGE 7

I love you even when you give me big, hairy, slobby kisses.

RUTH MILLER, AGE 8

The best thing about Grandpa is he Lets me Polish his head.

KATHRYN HEAD, AGE 8

KELLIE HUGHE[...]
AGE 11

Dear Grandpa,

I do not care how you look but who you are. To any other kid you are just an old man, but to me you are a kind old Grandad who I love too much for words.

I do not care if you are fat or slim,

I do not care if your hair is brown or white,

I do not care if you have blue eyes or brown.

All I care is that you're MY Grandad.

HELEN FIRTH, AGE 9

Silly Grandpa

I like you because you give me presents and you always fall asleep when you read me a story.

BEN HINER, AGE 6

And Grandad, you are funny like when you wash the clean dishes and don't wash the dirty dishes.

THOMAS PARTRIDGE, AGE 6

I love you because you are funny and you make me laugh. You mess around at the table. You tell me good jokes and you sit in your chair and look at a TV which isn't even turned on.

PETER STEVENSON, AGE 9

My Grand Dad is silly because he lets us have what we want.

TONI, AGE 9

Granda decided to have the car washed.
Pulling into the car wash Granda was shouting, "Emir! put your window up, Paul! sit down, Oonagh! close that door." The car wash started, water splashed into the car though, Guess whose window? Granda's!

SE SOUTAR,
AGE 7

EMIR SHEPPARD
AGE 11

Any time when your parents need a bit of time grandads are always there. Any time, Any day.

JAIMIE HARRIS, AGE 9

My grandfather is there whenever I need him, especially when I need to talk to him. He seems to understand more than our parents.

HEULWYN, AGE 12

CRAIG WALKER, AGE 7

Time for me

I love you Grandpa,
you're the best. I write
this piece for all you
have done for me over
the years, for caring
for me when I was ill
and for putting up
with me when
everyone is at work.
For keeping secrets
when I tell you them
and when I fall off my
bike you fix it.

PHILIP BELL, AGE 10

Our Secrets

Warning: do not read if of nervous disposure and do not show Grandma Please...

Dear Gramps, I like you because you did not tell Grandma about the tapioca pudding stain on the carpet beside the radiator

ALISTAIR ROBIN BOWDEN, AGE 9

I love you most when you share all your secrets with me like the time you told me you bent Daddy's bike wheel and blamed it on the cows.

CHRISTOPHER LAPPIN, AGE 11

I always tell my Grandfather secrets because I know he wont tell anybody else.

GREGORY KIRK, AGE 9

GRACE KING, AGE 9

Every valuable thing I would have I would give to you in return for every thing you gave me. and If you died I would be So Sad So Sad I would cry to death.

CHRISTOPHER LAPPIN, AGE 11

JASON MANZ, AGE 10

Stay by me

Dear Granda

I am writing to you to say I love you so
very, very much. I am sorry about the
time I sat on the table in your room and it
broke. Granda, I hope there is no noise in
Heaven because you did not like noise.

MARK JOHNSTON, AGE 10

My Grandad got a mesage,
from me it read:
"Dear Grandad
          I don,t want you
to go because you bring
warmth and comfort and I love
you, So Grandad did,nt go and
he brought warmth and
comfort.

ROBERT SIVELL, AGE 9

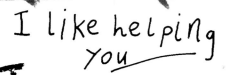

I like helping you

Thank you for letting me paint
your tractor red, Grandpa.
I wonder if I made a good job of it.
Grandpa, you said I did and told me
I was a good boy for helping you.
You painted the pipe and wheels. I
painted around the windows. I like
helping you, Grandpa. It is nice
being with you.

PAUL MCGUIRE, AGE 8

**Thank you for
letting me help
you**

MICHAEL.

KIMBERLEY DAVIDSON,
AGE 8

Old and beautiful

— X —

My Grandma
and Grandpa are
so caring
Their faces are
wrinkled but their
eyes are so
beautiful.

KELLY MARIE CASEY, AGE 7

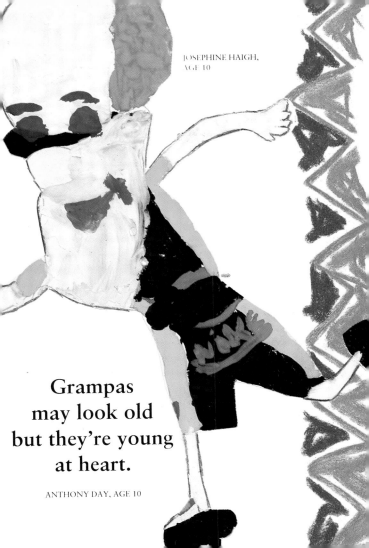

JOSEPHINE HAIGH,
AGE 10

**Grampas
may look old
but they're young
at heart.**

ANTHONY DAY, AGE 10

RACHEL
CARTWRIGHT.
AGE 6

My grandparents are a tonne of fun. If I ruled the world I'd give them a holiday every month, a load of money and pay their bills and make their home like a palace. Here's a message for everyone whose got grandparents - look after them.

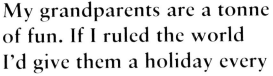

OMAR SROUJI, AGE 8

GARTH
SHIELDS,
AGE 6

If I ruled the world I'd give
my grandpa what he gave
me - love and kindness.

CHRISTOPHER MURRAY, AGE 10